Reader's Guides

Third Series

DETECTIVE FICTION

Compiled and Introduced by
W. B. STEVENSON

PUBLISHED FOR
THE NATIONAL BOOK LEAGUE
AT THE UNIVERSITY PRESS
CAMBRIDGE

1958

CAMBRIDGE UNIVERSITY PRESS
Cambridge, New York, Melbourne, Madrid, Cape Town,
Singapore, São Paulo, Delhi, Mexico City

Cambridge University Press
The Edinburgh Building, Cambridge CB2 8RU, UK

Published in the United States of America by Cambridge University Press, New York

www.cambridge.org
Information on this title: www.cambridge.org/9781107622210

© Cambridge University Press 1958

This publication is in copyright. Subject to statutory exception
and to the provisions of relevant collective licensing agreements,
no reproduction of any part may take place without the written
permission of Cambridge University Press.

First published 1958
Re-issued 2013

A catalogue record for this publication is available from the British Library

ISBN 978-1-107-62221-0 Paperback

Cambridge University Press has no responsibility for the persistence or
accuracy of URLs for external or third-party internet websites referred to in
this publication, and does not guarantee that any content on such websites is,
or will remain, accurate or appropriate.

CONTENTS

INTRODUCTION

As to old women and the majority of newspaper readers, they are pleased with anything as long as it is bloody enough. But the mind of sensibility requires something more.

—Thomas de Quincey

DETECTIVE FICTION has undergone considerable changes since the last NBL Reader's Guide on the subject was published in 1949. New writers have appeared, many of the older practitioners have ceased writing, many hundreds of novels have gone out of print: above all the novel of detection has changed in form in much the same way as contemporary fiction. There has been little diminution in the number of detective stories published. Nearly five hundred of them appear annually in Britain and America, and this total does not include paperback reprints. Although detective fiction continues to be neglected by the literary historians, it cannot be long before they take into account a form that has been popular for over a hundred years. Criticism of the detective story is taken a good deal more seriously than it was ten years ago, for few literary weeklies are without their column of reviews of new publications, while Francis Iles and Anthony Richardson in England, with Anthony Boucher and James Sandoe in America, bring to their criticisms standards as high as those held by their fellow reviewers of 'pure' literature. This guide sets out to indicate some trends in modern detective fiction, while pointing out some of the milestones on the road it has travelled.

The publication in English of DEE GOONG AN and the appearance this year of THE CHINESE BELL MURDERS may incline the future historian of detective fiction to credit the

Chinese with the invention of the form just as they have been credited with the invention of paper and explosives. Certainly these six eighteenth-century cases of Judge Dee have many of the characteristics of the modern detective story—the mysteries, the falsely accused persons, and the solutions arrived at by piecing clues together. It is equally certain that many such stories were in popular circulation in seventeenth- and eighteenth-century China. It would be less pedantic, however, to date the detective story from 1841, for in an issue of *Graham's Magazine* for that year appeared Edgar Allan Poe's 'The Murders in the Rue Morgue'. Auguste Dupin, with his learning and eccentricities, his intuition and his ' peculiar analytic ability ', is the father of the modern amateur detective. His successors were Sherlock Holmes and Philo Vance, Lord Peter Wimsey and Gervase Fen. The line of amateurs is dying out: the professionals and private investigators are taking their place.

The history of detective fiction, however, cannot be dealt with in this short introduction. The reader is referred to Howard Haycraft's well documented MURDER FOR PLEASURE which remains the most comprehensive history available. It can be supplemented by some of the books noted at the end of this list.

The continued popularity of detective fiction, the novel of crime and violence, in a world where violence is an everyday occurrence, must give rise to some speculation. Is the detective story merely a means of escape, a substitute for the fairy story ' the folk-myth of the twentieth century ' as C. Day Lewis suggests? Or is it, as Bertrand Russell writes ' an outlet for satisfying harmlessly the instincts we inherit from long generations of savages '? It is a fact that all kinds of people read detective stories—the don, the doctor, the clergyman, the technician and the scientist. Some of them read for relaxation, some for the thrill of the chase, others for the puzzle element: but all, surely, read them for the satisfaction of the deep seated instinct that right and wrong *do* exist, and that retribution certainly follows crime. The plots of detective stories are generally intricate, and this in itself is an additional satisfaction to readers weary of novels full of introspection and almost without plot.

What then constitutes the detective story? It must, first of all be logical and true to life, and it must keep to certain rules. The rules have been set down once and for all by Ronald Knox in his essay, ' Detective Decalogue '. The writer must be fair to the reader and the criminal must be introduced early in the book. All the detective's clues must be revealed, and as far as possible, his conclusions from them. The detective must not be the criminal. There must be no supernatural agencies introduced into the story, and no poisons unknown to science. There are prohibitions regarding twin brothers and sisters and too many secret passages. The rules are not hard and fast ones, and many eminent writers have broken one of them with telling effect. Agatha Christie's THE MURDER OF ROGER ACKROYD reveals the narrator as the criminal—but how satisfying and logical the story is! Even Sherlock Holmes concealed evidence and produced it triumphantly at the conclusion of the case. But few good writers break more than one rule at a time. It is possible, however, to ' invert ' the story and reveal the criminal at once, as did Francis Iles in MALICE AFORETHOUGHT or R. Austin Freeman in MR. POTTERMACK'S OVERSIGHT. The pattern of hunter and hunted is capable of a great deal of variation in the hands of a good craftsman. The rules, however, do exclude the shocker with its improbabilities, its heroes made of steel and rubber, its mysterious Chinese and its secret passages.

The ' thriller ' is more difficult to define. Probably Dorothy Sayers's dictum is best: that in the thriller the reader asks

'What happens next?', in the detective story 'What happened first?'. Thus the tale of pursuit or suspense (the form taken by so many modern novels) comes within the ambit of detective fiction, for we are generally asking 'why?'. The spy story, however, can generally be classed as a thriller. The definition is not, and cannot be an exact one: for there will always be 'borderline' stories such as Graham Greene's MINISTRY OF FEAR or Michael Innes's THE JOURNEYING BOY.

During the last ten years, detective fiction has gradually changed in form and content. The long and slow-paced puzzle story, dependent on alibis and timetables, has almost disappeared. The ingenious methods of murder have run through most of their permutations. The large house-party with its press of suspects is a thing of the past, and writers have had to strain their ingenuity to bring all their suspects together long enough for a crime to be committed. The 'butler did it' formula is finished, because there are few butlers left. In fact, detective fiction is becoming more realistic, and detectives instead of being changeless and seemingly immortal figures, are growing old and moving with the times. Raymond Chandler's scathing criticism of 'murder in an English rose-garden' may have had some effect, and the characters in the detective novel live in a modern, workaday world. As Miss Kay Dick has said ' Few detectives have time to sit down and think nowadays '.

One cannot doubt that this realism has come about through the impact of American fiction. In the stories of Hammett, Chandler and Macdonald action is the keynote and the narrative, written in a muscular prose, moves swiftly to a conclusion. Everything is seen through the eyes of the detective and the *denouements*, though surprising are always logical. The best of them as Gilbert Highet says ' come from the whole effort of the reader and the author working together'.

The imitators of the method are legion, and the formula rarely survives transportation across the Atlantic. But in their more sober British way, a similar realism is the foundation of the police stories of 'J. J. Marric' and Maurice Proctor, and the novels of John Trench.

A further change has come about. The cosy and talkative novel, with long stretches of conversation over the teacups, is being replaced by the tale of terror or pursuit. The study of criminal psychology has brought about a new attitude, and the ' had I but known ' story is almost a thing of the past. The most eminent practitioner in this new type of novel is Margaret Millar, whose A BEAST IN VIEW combines detection and terror in a virtuoso manner. John Bingham in his FIVE ROUNDABOUTS TO HEAVEN provides an equally convincing British study in the psychology of crime.

The list of authors that follows is an attempt at providing a basic list of writers of detective fiction. The first section of the list, THE OLD MASTERS, is a reminder of the pioneers of the form and authors of the present century who have ceased writing, but whose books are still satisfying. A number of writers mentioned in the previous Guide have been omitted, chiefly because so many of their books are out of print and difficult to obtain. The second part, THE MODERNS, includes those authors writing today from whom the reader may expect certain standards of logic, literacy, good plotting and characterisation. Their names have been chosen to exhibit the variety, freshness and vitality of modern detection. The list may seem to be a small one: it is a selection from possibly four hundred who have some claim to inclusion, and represents a choice made after much reading and consultation of authoritative criticism. The choice of individual books is the compiler's. It has not been possible to include in the limited space available more than a few authors who have only one or two outstanding books to their credit, or those who have published little during the last ten years. Such are Helen Eustis who has not provided us with a successor to her brilliant THE HORIZONTAL MAN, and Glyn Daniel, who writing as ' Dilwyn Rees ' has not followed up THE CAMBRIDGE MURDERS and WELCOME DEATH. In the second category are Anthony Boucher, H. C. Branson, Dorothy Hughes and Percival Wilde. Only the outstanding Continental detective—Simenon—appears in the list. One can note such single books as Catherine Arley's cynical WOMAN OF STRAW or the cold-blooded and ferocious THE LAW OF THE STREETS of Auguste le Breton. Also worth recording are the macabre tales of Boileau and Narcejac, or that curious Swiss incursion into crime, Friedrich Durrenmatt's THE JUDGE AND HIS HANGMAN. There are also crime writers in Germany, Japan and Mexico, but none of them are available in book form in Britain, though the curious may search for them in the pages of ELLERY QUEEN'S MYSTERY MAGAZINE.

Much detective fiction is written pseudonymously, many authors using two or three pen names, writing a different type of story under each. The Gardner-Fair alternate is now well known, but others may not be, and it is of interest to note such dual personalities as Crispin-Montgomery and Innes-Stewart, one a musician, the other a Shakespearian critic. All known pseudonyms have, therefore, been noted. The compiler has made much use of the writings of Howard Haycraft and Frederic Dannay. More personal acknowledgement is made to James Sandoe for his all-embracing knowledge of the American scene and his support and enthusiasm; and to Helene Zaiman for her notes on many years reading of detective fiction.

MENTIONED IN THE INTRODUCTION

Arley, Catherine, WOMAN OF STRAW. *Collins* 1957, 12s6d.

Bingham, J. FIVE ROUNDABOUTS TO HEAVEN. *Gollancz* 1953, 4s6d.

Christie, Agatha. THE MURDER OF ROGER ACKROYD. *Collins* 1926, 6s (*Fontana*), 2s6d.

Daniel, Glyn. WELCOME DEATH. *Gollancz* 1954, 10s6d.

Van Gulick, R. A., trans. DEE GOONG AN: three murder cases solved by Judge Dee. *Kegan Paul (Oriental Department)* 1949.

Van Gulick, R. A., trans. THE CHINESE BELL MURDERS. M. Joseph 1958, 13s6d.

Durrenmatt, F. THE JUDGE AND HIS HANGMAN. *Jenkins* 1954, 5s.

Eustis, H. THE HORIZONTAL MAN. *Hamilton* 1947.

Freeman, R. Austin. MR. POTTERMACK'S OVERSIGHT. *Hodder & Stoughton* 1930.

Greene, Graham. MINISTRY OF FEAR. *Heinemann* 1943, 8s6d.

Haycraft, H. MURDER FOR PLEASURE. *Davies* 1942, 15s.

Iles, F. MALICE AFORETHOUGHT. *Gollancz* 1931, 8s6d. *Pan*, 2s.

Innes, Michael. THE JOURNEYING BOY. *Gollancz* 1949, 6s.

Le Breton, A. THE LAW OF THE STREETS. *Collins* 1957, 10s6d.

Millar, Margaret. A BEAST IN VIEW. *Gollancz* 1955, 10s6d.

Rees, Dilwyn (Glyn Daniel). THE CAMBRIDGE MURDERS. *Gollancz* 1948; Penguin, 2s6d.

Reading List

All publishers are London firms except where otherwise stated. Dates of original publication are given; copies now available are in many cases later reprints. Prices (net and subject to alteration) are those prevailing in February 1958 and are given only where a book is known to be available new as this list goes to press.

THE OLD MASTERS

Bailey, H. C. THE BISHOP'S CRIME. *Gollancz* 1940.
Reginald Fortune, M.D., first appeared in CALL MR. FORTUNE (*Methuen* 1919), and Josiah Clunk in LITTLE CAPTAIN (*Gollancz* 1941; published in U.S.A as ORPHAN ANN).

Bentley, E. C. TRENT'S LAST CASE. *Nelson* 1913; new edn. 5*s.*; *Dent.*7*s6d*; Penguin 2*s6d*.
Philip Trent, connoisseur, is one of the earliest and most likeable of amateur detectives.

Berkeley, Anthony (Anthony Berkeley Cox). TRIAL AND ERROR. *Penguin* 1937, 2*s6d*.
A sound series of books, with Roger Sheringham as detective. The 'inverted' stories such as MALICE AFORETHOUGHT (*Gollancz* 1931, 8*s6d*; *Pan* 2*s.*) written under the name of Francis Iles are the best of their kind.

Bramah, Ernest (Ernest Bramah Smith). MAX CARRADOS MYSTERIES. *Hodder* 1927.
Bramah's blind detective worked by intuition and logical deduction, the stories have ingenuity and sound writing.

Brock, Lynn (Allister McAllister). THE STOAT. *Collins* 1940.
Slow-moving and absorbing: worthy of revival.

Chesterton, G. K. THE FATHER BROWN STORIES. *Cassell* 1947, 21*s.* FATHER BROWN SELECTED STORIES. *O.U.P.* (*World's Classics*) 1954, 6*s.*
Paradoxical, unexpected and original, these stories of the lovable priest rank as classics.

Connington, J. J. (Alfred Walter Stewart). DEATH AT SWAYTH-LING COURT. *Benn* 1926, 4s6d.
Sir Clinton Driffield, Chief Constable and breaker of ingenious alibis, is the detective.

Crofts, Freeman W. SIR JOHN MAGILL'S LAST JOURNEY *Penguin* 1930.
Trains and timetables figure prominently in his complicated puzzle stories. THE CASK (*Collins* 1920) remains a landmark.

Doyle, *Sir* Arthur Conan. SHERLOCK HOLMES COMPLETE SHORT STORIES; COMPLETE LONG STORIES. *Murray* 1928, 1929, each 18s. SELECTED STORIES. *O.U.P.* (*World's Classics*) 1951, 7s.
' More than a book—he is the spirit of a town and a time ' (Hector Bolitho).

Collins, Wilkie. THE MOONSTONE *Tinsley* 1868; *Dent* (*Everyman*) 1957, 8s6d.; *Penguin* 3s6d.; *Collins* (*Classics*) 5s6d.; *O.U.P.* (*World's Classics*) 6s.
' The first, the longest and the best of English detective stories ' (T. S. Eliot).

Freeman, R. Austin. THE DOCTOR THORNDYKE OMNIBUS. *Hodder* 1929, 18s.
John Thorndyke, K.C. was the foremost of scientific detectives, appearing first in THE RED THUMB MARK (1911). The ' inverted ' stories such as MR. POTTERMACK'S OVERSIGHT (1930) should not be forgotten.

Gaboriau, Emile. THE WIDOW LEROUGE (1866), *Vizetelly* 1885.
The pioneer among French writers, with M. Lecoq his most famous detective.

Green, Anna Katherine. THE LEAVENWORTH CASE. *Putnam* 1878.
The first American detective novel.

Hammett, Dashiell. THE DASHIELL HAMMETT OMNIBUS. *Cassell* 1952, 21s.
' Every character is trying to deceive all the others . . . the truth slowly becomes visible through the haze of deception ' (André Gide). This volume includes Hammett's masterpieces THE MALTESE FALCON (1930) and THE GLASS KEY (1931).

Knox, Ronald A. FOOTSTEPS AT THE LOCK. *Methuen* 1928, 6*s*.
Miles Bredon, insurance investigator, appears in six excellent stories. This is the only one now in print.

McGuire, Paul. THE SPANISH STEPS. *Heinemann* 1940.
A much neglected writer worthy of revival.

Mason, A. E. W. INSPECTOR HANAUD INVESTIGATES. *Hodder* 1931, 21*s*.
AT THE VILLA ROSE (1912) and other cases of Inspector Hanaud, are among the best of their time.

Morrison, Arthur. MARTIN HEWITT, INVESTIGATOR. *Ward Lock* 1894.
Although fifty years old, many of these pioneer stories retain their charm.

Poe, Edgar Allan. TALES OF MYSTERY AND IMAGINATION *Dent (Everyman)* 1908, 7*s*.
Auguste Dupin, the most original of all private investigators, first appeared in 1841. Poe remains the first great master of the detective short story.

Post, Melville Davisson. UNCLE ABNER. *Appleton, N.Y.* 1918.
Long out of print, these early stories have reappeared in ELLERY QUEEN'S MYSTERY MAGAZINE (*Mellifont Press*).

Sayers, Dorothy L. THE NINE TAILORS. *Gollancz* 1934.
Scrupulous writing and authentic backgrounds are the foundations for the Lord Peter Wimsey stories, of which the above is the finest.

Van Dine, S. S. (Willard Huntingdon Wright). THE BISHOP MURDER CASE. *Benn* 1929.
Philo Vance, the man about town, figures in many complicated cases. The above and THE GREENE MURDER CASE (1927) are free from the authors later mannerisms.

THE MODERNS

Allingham, Margery (Mrs. Philip Youngman Carter). FLOWERS FOR THE JUDGE. *Heinemann* 1946, 8*s*6*d*.; *Penguin* 2*s*6*d*.
Good writing, fairness to the reader, and a delightful sense of humour make Miss Allingham's tales of Albert Campion outstanding.

Armstrong, Charlotte (Mrs. J. Lewi). MISCHIEF. *Peter Davies* 1951; *Penguin 2s6d.*
There is an agreeable tinge of cold grue in the above and the author's subsequent novels of terror.

Bagby, George, *see* Stein, Aaron Marc.

Bax, Roger, *see* Garve, Anthony.

Bell, Josephine (Mrs. N. D. Ball). BONES IN THE BARROW. *Methuen* 1953.
Dr. David Wintringham and Inspector Mitchell are featured in a series of sober, intelligent novels.

Bell, Vicars Walker. DEATH AND THE NIGHT WATCHES. *Faber* 1955, 6s.
These well-written stories have rural settings, befitting the chronicler of LITTLE GADDESDEN (*Faber* 1949, 12s6d.).

Bellairs, George. DEATH DROPS THE PILOT. *Gifford* 1956, 10s6d.
Long by modern standards, the detections of Inspector Little-john are closely and absorbingly written.

Bingham, John Michael Ward. FIVE ROUNDABOUTS TO HEAVEN. *Gollancz* 1953, 4s6d.
Tense stories of retribution equipped with skilfully engineered climaxes.

Blake, Nicholas (Cecil Day Lewis). THERE'S TROUBLE BREWING. *Collins* 1937; (*Fontana*) 1956, 2s.
Some of the most brilliantly written detective stories of today, which feature Nigel Strangeways, with END OF CHAPTER (*Collins* 1957, 12s6d.) his latest case.

Brand, Christianna (Mrs. Mary Christianna Lewis). GREEN FOR DANGER. *Bodley Head* 1945.
Inspector Cockrill figures in a series of witty and lightly written novels.

Brean, Herbert. THE CLOCK STRIKES THIRTEEN. *Heinemann* 1954.
An able recruit to the John Dickson Carr school, with his own blend of original situations.

Bush, Christopher. THE CASE OF THE TUDOR QUEEN. *Penguin* 1938, 2*s*6*d*.
Ludovic Travers and Superintendent Wharton are the detectives in Bush's many ingenious, sobersided stories.

Candy, Edward (Allison Neville). BONES OF CONTENTION. *Gollancz* 1952.
There is some witty writing in her three novels of crime among the doctors.

Cannan, Joanna (Mrs. H. J. Pullein-Thompson). LONG SHADOWS. *Gollancz* 1955.
The few detective stories written by this able novelist are worthy of revival.

Carnac, Carol, *see* Lorac, E. C. R.

Carr, John Dickson. HAG'S NOOK. *Hamish Hamilton* 1933.
Whether writing under his own name about Dr. Gideon Fell, or as ' Carter Dickson ' about Sir Henry Merrivale, the author is the virtuoso of the locked room or the ' impossible murder '. The historical detective stories such as FIRE, BURN (*Hamish Hamilton* 1957, 13*s*6*d*.) should be noted.

Chandler, Raymond. FAREWELL MY LOVELY. *Hamish Hamilton* 1940, 6*s*.; *Penguin* 2*s*6*d*.
' Rude wit, a lively sense of the grotesque, a disgust for sham, and a contempt for pettiness ' are the characteristics of Philip Marlowe, the author's detective, who appears in seven outstanding books.

Christie, Agatha (Mrs. A. C. Mallowan). THE MURDER OF ROGER ACKROYD. *Collins* 1926, 6*s*; (*Fontana*) 2*s*6*d*.
The supreme conjurer of the detective novel, whose solutions never disappoint and always surprise, and have continued to do so for over thirty years.

Claymore, Tod (Hugh Clevely). NEST OF VIPERS. *Penguin* 1948, 2*s*6*d*.
Fast-moving first person singular novels, by an English recruit to the Chandler school.

Crispin, Edmund (Robert Bruce Montgomery). LOVE LIES BLEEDING. *Penguin* 1948.
Fantastic and sophisticated, these novels about Gervase Fen, an Oxford don, are witty, and unexpected in their solutions.

Curtiss, Ursula. THE IRON COBWEB. *Eyre & Spottiswoode* 1954, 6s.
' A deft arrangement of little terrors juggled into a great big fear ' (Sandoe). This is the third of the author's stories.

Daly, Elizabeth. EVIDENCE OF THINGS SEEN. *Hammond* 1946, 6s.
Henry Gamadge, bibliophile, is the detective in many well-written books.

Davis, Dorothy Salisbury. DEATH OF AN OLD SINNER. *Secker* 1958, 12s6d.
Irony is the chief characteristic of this able writer; hitherto her books have only been available in paperback editions.

Dickson, Carter, *see* Carr, John Dickson.

Dillon, Eilis (Mrs. Cormac O. Cuilleanain). SENT TO HIS ACCOUNT. *Faber* 1954, 6s.
Charming stories written by an Irishwoman, equally notable for her children's books.

Dodge, David. BULLETS FOR THE BRIDEGROOM. *M. Joseph* 1948; *Penguin 2s6d.*
An author who writes detective stories and thrillers, and is successful in both. His detective James Whitney, a public accountant, is tough and unscrupulous.

Ellin, Stanley. MYSTERY STORIES. *Boardman* 1957 11s6d.
A sparkling newcomer, discovered by ELLERY QUEEN'S MYSTERY MAGAZINE, whose short stories have more than a tinge of the macabre.

Farrer, Katharine. THE MISSING LINK. *Collins* 1952; *Penguin 2s6d.*
Learned, ingenious and amusing, the above and THE CRETAN COUNTERFEIT (*Collins* 1954 6s.) strike a new note.

Fearing, Kenneth. THE LONELIEST GIRL IN THE WORLD. *Bodley Head* 1952.
This American poet has written infrequently, but his ' borderline ' novels are unusual, the above and DAGGER OF THE MIND (1941) being most notable.

Ferrars, Elizabeth (Morna D. Brown) REMOVE THE BODIES. *Penguin* 1940, 2s6d.
Toby Dyke does the reasoning and George, ex-burglar, the investigation and hard work.

Finnegan, Robert. THE BANDAGED NUDE. *Penguin* 1949, 2s6d.
A crime reporter, Don Banion, is featured in some tough minded and fast-moving tales.

Finney, Jack. FIVE AGAINST THE HOUSE. *Eyre & Spottiswoode* 1954, 10s6d.
A story of a perfect crime that went wrong, by an author with three good books to his credit.

Fitt, Mary (Mrs. Kathleen Freeman). CLUES TO CHRISTOBEL. *M. Joseph* 1944.
The author is a classical scholar, and has written many subtle and original stories, with Dr. Fitzbrown and Superintendent Mallett as detectives. SWEET POISON (*Macdonald* 1956, 10s6d.) is a good recent example.

Fitzgerald, Nigel. MIDSUMMER MALICE. *Collins* 1953; (*Fontana*) 2s.
The author's tales are set in Eire, with a charming actor as private investigator. Feckless characters and exciting climaxes abound.

Ford, Leslie, *see* Frome, David.

Fox, James M. (J. M. W. Knipscheer). CODE THREE. *Hammond* 1956, 10s6d.
His police stories are more neatly tailored than those concerning private detective James Marshall.

Frome, David (Mrs. Zenith Jones Brown). THE HAMMERSMITH MURDERS. *Methuen* 1930.
We have heard little recently of Mr. Pinkerton, a shy and unassuming detective, though the author continues to write under her ' Leslie Ford ' pseudonym.

Fuller, Roy. THE SECOND CURTAIN. *Deutsch* 1953, 5s.
A grim story of pursuit coming from an outstanding poet.

Gardner, Erle Stanley. THE CASE OF THE DUBIOUS BRIDE-GROOM. *Heinemann* 1954, 5s.; *Pan*, 2s.
Perry Mason, the ever-young criminal lawyer has figured in many cases; they are of standard brand, surprising in their courtroom climaxes. The ' A.A. Fair ' stories about Bertha Cool and Donald Lam are of tougher fibre, with BEDROOMS HAVE WINDOWS (*Heinemann* 1956, 12s6d.) a good example.

Garve, Andrew (Paul Winterton). DEATH AND THE SKY ABOVE. *Collins* 1953; *Pan*, 2s.
The author is prolific, reliable and ingenious. His MURDER IN MOSCOW (*Collins* 1951) comes from his experience as a foreign correspondent, and his ' Roger Bax ' pseudonym should be noted.

Gilbert, Anthony (Lucy Beatrice Malleson). RIDDLE OF A LADY. *Collins* 1956, 6s.
Arthur Crook, a solicitor, sails close to the wind, but he prevents crimes as well as solving them. ' Anne Meredith' is an alternate pseudonym for a series of ' inverted ' crime stories.

Gilbert, Michael Francis. SMALLBONE DECEASED. *Hodder* 1950, 6s.
A prominent writer of the younger generation, equally at home in the thriller: his scrupulous detail betokens his legal experience.

Graaf, Peter. DAUGHTER FAIR. *M. Joseph* 1958, 13s6d.
Joe Dust, a tough and cynical American, has set up as an English ' private eye '. The results in the above and DUST AND THE CURIOUS BOY (*M. Joseph* 1957) are promising.

Hall, Oakley Maxwell, *see* Manor, Jason.

Hare, Cyril (Alfred Alexander Gordon Clark). TRAGEDY AT LAW. *Faber* 1942, 6s6d.
The author is a judge, with nine fastidiously written stories to his credit, the latest being HE SHOULD HAVE DIED HERE-AFTER (*Faber* 1958, 12s6d.).

19

Head, Matthew (John Edwin Canaday). MURDER AT THE FLEA CLUB. *Heinemann* 1957, 13*s*6*d*.

Dr. Mary Finney deserts Leopoldville to solve a case in the bistros and nightclubs of Paris. The author has an incisive style and a keen ironic sense.

Heyer, Georgette (Mrs. George R. Rougier). ENVIOUS CASCA. *Heinemann* 1941, 7*s*6*d*.

More famous for her historical novels, the author has written some unusual detective stories.

Hull, Richard (Richard Henry Simpson). KEEP IT QUIET. *Penguin* 1935, 2*s*6*d*.

Rather uneven in performance, his earlier books, such as the above and MURDER ISN'T EASY (*Faber* 1936) are the best.

Iams, Jack. A CORPSE OF THE OLD SCHOOL. *Gollancz* 1955, 10*s*6*d*.

Alcohol-laden, funny and furious, his novels are not for the purist.

Iles, Francis, *see* Berkeley, Anthony.

Innes, Michael (John Innes Mackintosh Stewart). HAMLET, REVENGE. *Gollancz* 1937, 8*s*6*d*.

John Appleby has risen to Knighthood and an Assistant Commissioner's post since his earliest cases. He remains the delight of connoisseurs.

Irish, William (George Hopley). THE NIGHT I DIED. *Hutchinson* 1954.

Fear is the keynote in his stories of suspense. The books written under his own name and that of ' Cornell Woolrich ' are worth seeking out.

Jay, Charlotte [Geraldine]. THE FUGITIVE EYE. *Collins* 1953; *White Circle* 2*s*.

An apt exponent of the tale of terror.

Latimer, Jonathan. SINNERS AND SHROUDS. *Methuen* 1956, 12*s*6*d*.

His detectives are dissolute and drunken, but get there in the end.

Lawrence, Hilda. DEATH OF A DOLL. *Penguin* 1948, 2s6d.
Quietly terrifying stories of detective Mark East.

Lockridge, Frances and Richard. DEAD AS A DINOSAUR.
Hutchinson 1956, 10s6d.
A curious duo; for F. and R. write of Mr. and Mrs. North,
R. and F. of Lieutenant Heimrich—their stories are of the
sophisticated *New Yorker* type.

Lorac, E. C. R. (Edith Caroline Rivett). POLICEMEN IN THE
PRECINCT. *Collins* 1949.
The Inspector Macdonald stories are many, and soundly
constructed. The tales written under her ' Carol Carnac '
pseudonym, such as DOUBLE TURN (*Collins* 1956, 10s6d.),
have more of a feminine appeal.

McCloy, Helen (Mrs. Davis Dresser). THE ONE THAT GOT
AWAY. *Gollancz* 1954.
Basil Willing, psychiatrist, is an interesting character, and the
stories about him are subtle, exciting and well-written.

Macdonald, John Ross (Kenneth Millar). FIND A VICTIM. *Cassell*
1955, 5s.
The author is of the Hammett-Chandler school. Archer, his
detective, has a rock-like integrity and toughness, and the
stories a ruthless brilliance.

Macdonald, Philip. THE NOOSE. *Collins* 1930; (*Fontana*) 2s.
His early stories about Anthony Gethryn and the outstanding
X v. REX (*Collins* 1933) are brisk, exciting and logical.

McGerr, Pat. YOUR LOVING VICTIM. *Collins* 1951.
More interesting for their ' gimmicks ' than their logic, with
PICK YOUR VICTIM (1947) and the above as good examples of
their kind.

McGivern, William P. THE BIG HEAT. *Hamish Hamilton* 1953;
Penguin 2s6d.
Novels of crime and racketeers in New York, generally with a
lone wolf policeman as central character.

Mackinnon, Allan. MURDER, REPEAT, MURDER. *Collins* 1952.
Stanner and McCallum are the C.I.D. men in a soundly
constructed series.

21

Mainwaring, Margaret. MURDER IN PASTICHE. *Gollancz* 1955.
A delicious absurdity, with nine thinly disguised amateur
detectives solving a murder in nine different ways.

Manor, Jason (Oakley Maxwell Hall). THE TRAMPLERS. *Secker*
1951, 11s6d.
Politics, rackets and murder in California, described in the
Chandler tradition. The author's CORPUS OF JOE BAILEY
(*Reinhardt* 1953) written under his real name, should be noted.

Marric, J. J. (John Creasey). GIDEON'S DAY. *Hodder* 1955, 10s6d.;
Pan 2s6d.
Commander George Gideon of Scotland Yard is a sterling
character, and his days and nights are full of action.

Marsh, Ngaio. DEATH IN A WHITE TIE. *Bles* 1938, 5s.
A New Zealand woman writer of rare ability, scrupulously fair
to the reader: her detective Roderick Alleyn grows old
gracefully.

Millar, Margaret. A BEAST IN VIEW. *Gollancz* 1955, 2s6d.
Superb tales of terror, written by the wife of 'John Ross
Macdonald'.

Miller, Wade (Bob Wade and Bill Miller). SHOOT TO KILL.
Museum Press 1953.
The Max Thursday books are rough, but scrupulous in their
fairness to the reader.

Mitchell, Gladys. COME AWAY DEATH. *Penguin* 1937.
Dame Beatrice Lestrange Bradley is one of the most likeable
women detectives, figuring in some complicated plots.

Mole, William (William Younger). SKIN TRAP. *Eyre & Spottiswoode* 1957, 12s6d.
Casson Duker, the author's wine-merchant detective, co-
operates with the police in some excellent cases.

Murray, Max. THE KING AND THE CORPSE. *M. Joseph* 1951;
Penguin 2s6d.
Witty and sophisticated stories, unorthodox in form, by an
author who died too young.

Nielsen, Helen. THE WOMAN ON THE ROOF. *Gollancz* 1955, 10s6d.
A clever combination of detection and pursuit, set in a Los Angeles bungalow court. Miss Nielsen is a new writer of some promise.

Offord, Lenore Glen. THE SMILING TIGER. *Jarrolds* 1951, 6s.
Her stories are quietly sinister with good characterisation.

Page, Marco (Harry Kurnitz). RECLINING FIGURE. *Eyre & Spottiswoode* 1952, 6s.
Artists, authors and booksellers perform in some amiable mix-ups.

Piper, Evelyn. BUNNY LAKE IS MISSING. *Secker* 1958, 12s6d.
The author is one of the most able writers of the tale of pursuit. Her earlier book THE INNOCENT (*Boardman* 1951), is worth seeking out.

Postgate, Raymond. SOMEBODY AT THE DOOR. *M. Joseph* 1943.
The above, VERDICT OF TWELVE (*Penguin*, 2s6d.) and THE LEDGER IS KEPT (*M. Joseph* 1953), are mordant, difficult to forget, and too few for the devotee.

Potts, Jean. GO, LOVELY ROSE. *Gollancz* 1955, 10s6d.
The debut of an unusually talented author of suspense stories who has a sense of character and climax.

Procter, Maurice. THE CHIEF INSPECTOR'S STATEMENT. *Hutchinson* 1951.
Realistic and tersely written stories of crooks and police work written by an ex-policeman.

Punshon, E. R. DEATH AMONG THE SUNBATHERS. *Penguin* 1934.
With nearly fifty years of writing to his credit, the author remains scrupulous, painstaking and soberly detailed.

Queen, Ellery (Frederic Dannay and Manfred B. Lee). THE ROMAN HAT MYSTERY. *Penguin* 1929, 2s6d.
A scintillant collaboration whose books are complicated, mystifying and satisfying. Their services to the detective short story are outstanding, the chief of them being the anthologies published as ELLERY QUEEN'S MYSTERY MAGAZINE (*Mellifont Press*) and ELLERY QUEEN'S AWARDS (*Collins*, tenth and eleventh series each 12s6d.; 9th series 6s.).

Quentin, Patrick (Richard W. Webb and Hugh C. Wheeler). THE MAN WITH TWO WIVES. *Gollancz* 1955, 10s6d.
Two collaborators who keep up a high standard under three pseudonyms. Their ' Jonathan Stagge ' stories such as DEATH'S OLD SWEET SONG (*M. Joseph* 1947, 4s6d.) incline to the supernatural. The ' Q. Patrick ' stories about Lieutenant Trant are all out of print.

Rhode, John (C. J. C. Street). AN ARTIST DIES. *Bles* 1956, 6s.
His first story A.S.F. dates from 1924. Professor Priestley and Inspector Jimmy Waghorn continue to provide the solutions to many entertaining puzzles.

Rice, Craig. THE FOURTH POSTMAN. *Hammond* 1948 6s.
Zany stories, with J. J. Malone solving the cases through a mist of alcohol and cigar smoke.

Roth, Holly. SHADOW OF A LADY. *Hamish Hamilton* 1957, 12s6d.
Quiet and careful writing, paradoxical endings, are the features of Miss Roth's outstanding tales.

Seeley, Mabel. THE LISTENING HOUSE. *Collins* 1939.
The foremost exponent of the ' had I but known ' school, with the above and THE STRANGER BESIDE ME (*Muller* 1953) her most noteworthy books.

Simenon, Georges. MAIGRET RIGHT AND WRONG. *Hamish Hamilton* 1954, 7s6d.
Solid, humane and implacable, Inspector Maigret is the most convincing of French detectives. Simenon's stories have a Gallic worldliness and grim realism.

Smith, Shelley (Nancy Bodington). MAN ALONE. *Collins* 1952; *White Circle* 2s.
Miss Smith is adept at screwing up nervous tension, the above being a realistic story of a petty criminal.

Spicer, Bart. THE DARK LIGHT. *Collins* 1950.
His detective Carney Wilde prowls the back-streets of crime, yet has humanity and compassion.

Stagge, Jonathan, *see* Quentin, Patrick.

Stein, Aaron Marc (Hampton Stone). THE CORPSE THAT REFUSED TO STAY DEAD. *Dobson* 1954.
A ' triple-threat ' writer who under his own name writes archaeological-detective stories such as MOONMILK AND MURDER (*Macdonald* 1956, 6*s*.). The ' George Bagby ' stories like THE BODY IN THE BASKET (*Macdonald* 1956) are police tales of New York.

Stout, Rex. BEFORE MIDNIGHT. *Collins* 1956, 6*s*.
Nero Wolfe, fat and immobile, and his tough secretary Archie Goodwin are an inimitable pair: the stories are cut to a pattern, but never dull.

Symons, Julian. THE NARROWING CIRCLE. *Gollancz* 1954.
Characterisation, atmosphere and good writing distinguish his books, with BLAND BEGINNING (*Collins* 1949; *White Circle* 2*s*.) presenting a bibliographical case with echoes of the Wise forgeries.

Tey, Josephine (Elizabeth Mackintosh). THE FRANCHISE AFFAIR. *Peter Davies* 1948, 10*s*6*d*.; *Penguin* 2*s*6*d*.
Better known as ' Gordon Daviot ' the playwright, her crime novels were substantial and well-written. The above is an ingenious re-telling of the Elizabeth Canning mystery in a modern setting.

Trench, John. WHAT ROUGH BEAST. *Macdonald* 1957, 10*s*6*d*.
The third novel by an outstanding new writer. His archaeologist-detective Cotterell frequently finds himself in conflict with the police; his methods are painstaking and absorbing to the reader.

Upfield, Arthur W. THE BATTLING PROPHET. *Heinemann* 1956, 12*s*6*d*.
The half-aboriginal Detective Inspector Napoleon Bonaparte figures in many strange stories of the outbacks of Australia: he is unique.

Vickers, Roy. THE DEPARTMENT OF DEAD ENDS. *Penguin* 1949, 2*s*6*d*.
Short stories of unsolved crimes, patiently unravelled by Scotland Yard: old-fashioned writing, but absorbing detection. MURDERING MR. VELFRAGE (*Faber* 1950) is a worthy successor to the above.

Wade, Henry (*Sir* H. L. Aubrey-Fletcher). BE KIND TO THE KILLER. *Constable* 1952, 6s.
The chronicles of Inspector Poole are soberly written, detailed, yet never dull.

Walsh, Thomas. NIGHT WATCH. *Hamish Hamilton* 1952.
An American writer, whose sombre stories of police routine in New York have exciting climaxes.

Waugh, Hillary. LAST SEEN WEARING . . . *Gollancz* 1953, 9s6d.
The best of a number of novels of breathless excitement.

Witting, Clifford. MIDSUMMER MURDER *Hodder* 1937, 2s.
Inspector Charlton and Detective Peter Bradfield cope quietly and competently with crime in Downshire.

BOOKS ABOUT DETECTIVE FICTION

Carter, John. COLLECTING DETECTIVE FICTION. *Constable* 1938.
A learned essay for the bibliophile.

Haycraft, Howard. MURDER FOR PLEASURE: the life and times of the detective story. *Peter Davies* 1942.
The best history of the detective story, with valuable check lists and an extensive bibliography.

Haycraft, Howard, ed. THE ART OF THE MYSTERY STORY: a collection of critical essays. *Simon & Schuster, N.Y.* 1946.
An invaluable collection, including Chandler's ' Simple Art of Murder ', Knox's ' Detective Decalogue ', S. S. Van Dine's ' The Great Detective Stories ', and many other essays by practitioners and critics.

Hogarth, Basil. WRITING THRILLERS FOR PROFIT. *A. & C. Black* 1936.

Morland, Nigel. HOW TO WRITE DETECTIVE NOVELS. *Allen & Unwin* 1936.

Queen, Ellery. QUEEN'S QUORUM. *Gollancz* 1953.
The 101 best books of detective stories, with commentary.

Queen, Ellery, ed. ELLERY QUEEN'S AWARDS *Gollancz*, series 1–7, 1946–1954; *Collins*, 9th series 6*s*.; 10th and 11th series each 12*s*6*d*.
Prize winning stories from ELLERY QUEEN'S MYSTERY MAGAZINE with commentaries on the authors.

Sayers, Dorothy L. GREAT SHORT STORIES OF DETECTION MYSTERY AND HORROR. *Gollancz*, Series 1–3 (6 parts) 1928–1934, 6*s*6*d* to 10*s*6*d*.
Contain superb introductions, forming a miniature history.

Scott, Sutherland. BLOOD IN THEIR INK. *Stanley Paul* 1953.
A history written with some gusto, but uneven in treatment.

Thomas, Gilbert. HOW TO ENJOY DETECTIVE FICTION. *Rockliff* 1947.
Attempts to do too much, but is informed and enthusiastic.

Thomson, H. Douglas. MASTERS OF MYSTERY: a study of the detective story. *Collins* 1931.
Out of print, out of date, but still of interest.

Wrong, E. M., ed. CRIME AND DETECTION. *O.U.P.* (*World's Classics*) 1926.
Contains a valuable introduction.

INDEX OF TITLES

Lightning Source UK Ltd.
Milton Keynes UK
UKHW020749060819
347479UK00006B/186/P

9 781107 622210